Withdrawn

Alexandria-Monroe
Public Library
117 East Church Street
Alexandria, IN 46001-2005

this book belongs to

_____

by Yaffa Ganz

illustrations: Harvey Klineman

FELDHEIM PUBLISHERS Jerusalem / New York

Alexandria-Monroe
Public Library
117 East Church Street
Alexandria, IN 46001-2005

Me and my Bubby, my Zeidy and me

Library of Congress Cataloging-in-Publication Data

Ganz, Yaffa,
Me and my bubby, my zeidy and me / by Yaffa Ganz; illustrated by Harvey Klineman.
36 p. 22 cm.
Summary: Depicts the special relationship that children share with their grandparents by showing them participating in a variety of activities involving Jewish tradition and culture.
ISBN 0-87306-543-3
1. Grandparents--Juvenile literature. 2. Jews--Families--Juvenile literature.
3. Jews--Social life and customs--Juvenile literature.
[1. Grandparents. 2. Jews--Social life and customs.] I. Klineman, Harvey, ill.
II. Title.
HQ759.9.G36   1990
306.874'5'088296--dc20   90-38307
                                                                    CIP
                                                                    AC

First published 1990

Copyright © 1990 by Yaffa Ganz

No part of this publication may be translated, reproduced, stored in a retrieval system or transmitted, in any form or by any means, electronic, mechanical, photocopying, recording or otherwise, without prior permission in writing from the publishers.

Philipp Feldheim Inc.
200 Airport Executive Park
Spring Valley, NY 10977

Printed in Israel

For
my Bubby
Blima
and
my Bubby
Gittel
ע״ה

and for
my Zeidys
**Velvel,
Yaakov,**
and
**Shaul
haLevi**
ז״ל

Bubbys and zeidys are very special people. We have two of each. Bubby Debby and Zeidy Gershon are Mommy's parents. Bubby Feygie and Zeidy Shlomo are Daddy's parents. That's us, there in the middle.

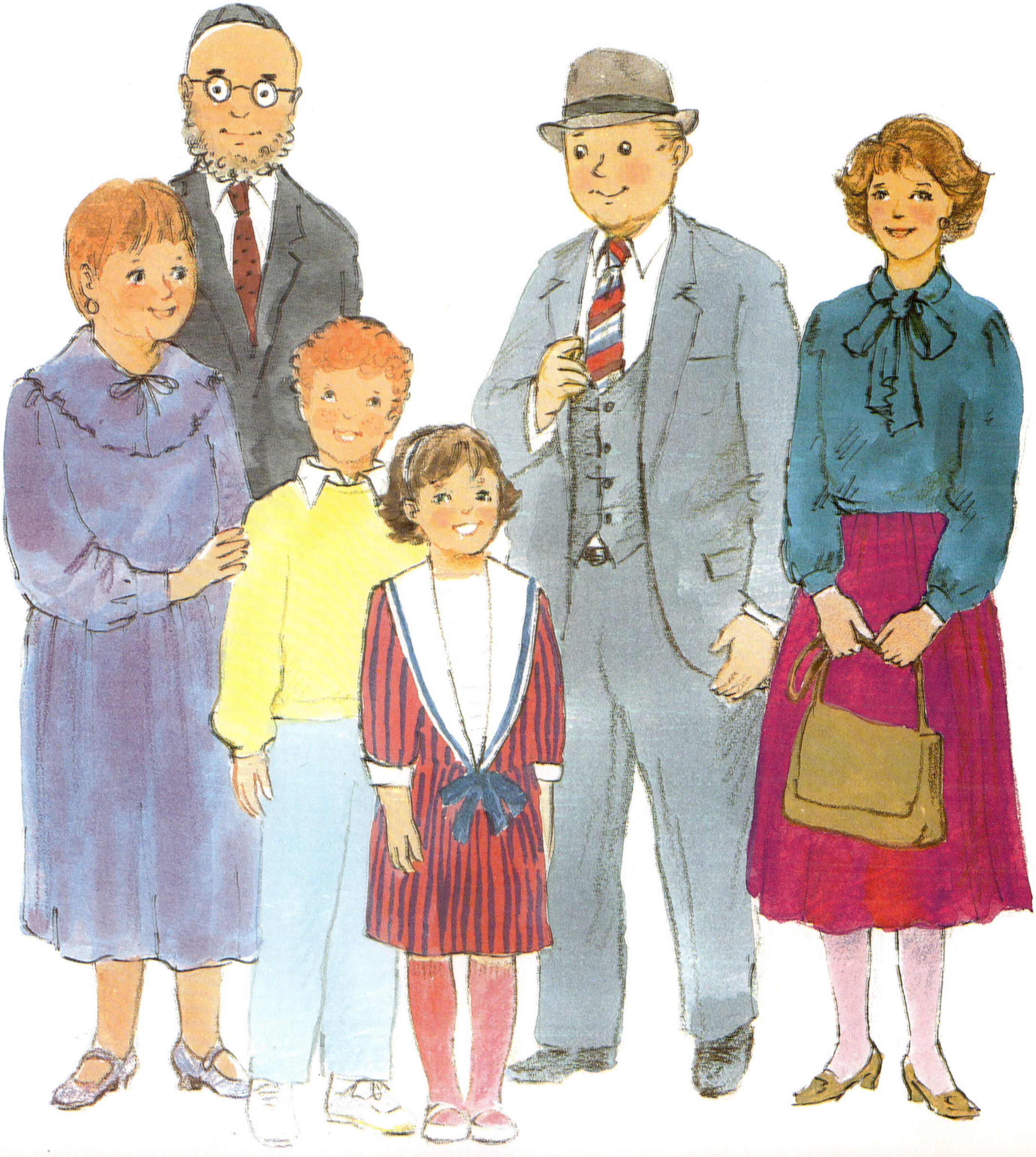

Bubby's mother came to America on a crowded boat when she was only twelve years old. She brought her mother's big Shabbos candlesticks with her. Bubby still uses them every Friday night.
When I'm grown-up, Bubby says I can have them.

Zeidy's father was a soldier in the Russian army, but he didn't want to fight. There were Jewish soldiers in the army they were fighting against, and Zeidy's father didn't want to hurt them.

Bubby always has something interesting for me when she comes to visit — stickers, stamps, magic markers, bubble gum or funny key rings. She never comes with an empty purse. And if I'm sick, she knows just how to make my medicine taste good, and how to make my sore throat or fever go away. She's better than the doctor!

Zeidy makes toys from the things he finds in his pockets. My favorite is his Handkerchief Mouse. It has ears and a tail. You should see how Zeidy makes it jump! When I'm sick, Zeidy comes to keep me company.

He says I'm such a troublemaker that someone has to keep an eye on me, even if I'm in bed. But he doesn't really mean it.

Every Thursday, Bubby makes challa for Shabbos. I love to watch her knead the dough. When it's ready, she lets me make the braids. Then we cut off a piece of dough and burn it to perform the mitzvah of "challa".

Each one of Zeidy's grandchildren gets his or her own special Shabbos blessing on Friday nights. We all line up — the oldest first, the youngest last — and wait our turn. I wouldn't miss Zeidy's bracha for anything.

My friends and I were playing jump rope and we asked Bubby if she wanted to play. She was willing to turn, but she said she's too old to jump. I don't think Bubby is old.

Zeidy used to be a great baseball player, but last spring, when we asked him to be on our team, he said he'd rather be the umpire. He said it takes too much energy to run around all those bases. I guess he was tired that day.

Bubby doesn't talk much in shul, but she smiles at me a lot, even when she's davening. And she helps me keep the place in my siddur.

I love to watch Zeidy when he reads in the Sefer Torah. He pulls his big white tallis over his head, bends over the Torah, and sways back and forth. You can hear every single word when Zeidy reads. I learned the melody just by listening to him.

Bubby does a lot of Pesach shopping, so I usually go with her to help. I push the cart and she fills it up. When it gets too heavy for me, she pushes and I put the food in. Bubby always buys me something good to eat before we leave the supermarket.

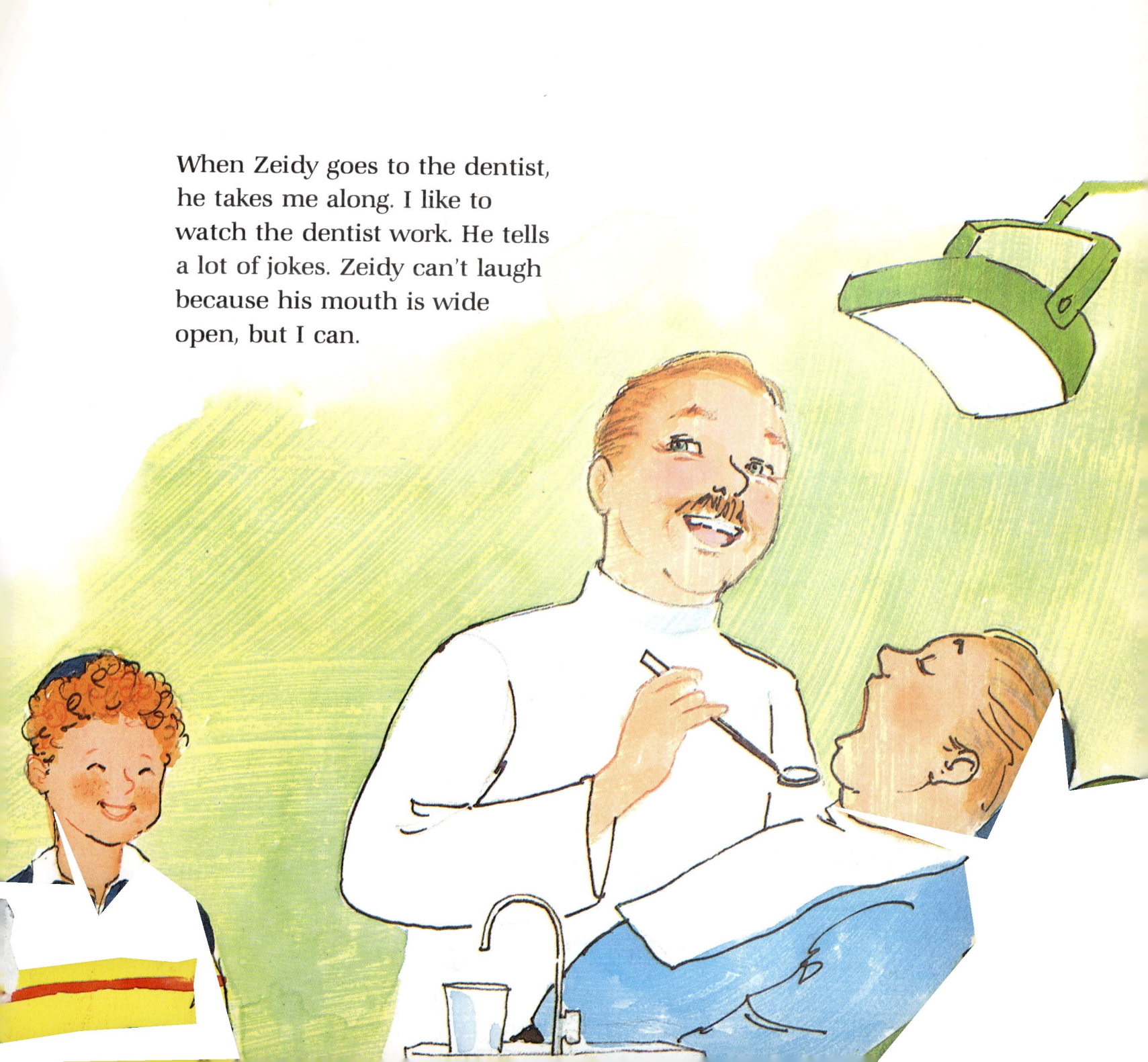

When Zeidy goes to the dentist, he takes me along. I like to watch the dentist work. He tells a lot of jokes. Zeidy can't laugh because his mouth is wide open, but I can.

Every morning, especially in the winter, Bubby feeds the birds. She puts out crumbs for them on her back porch. She feeds stray cats too. One spring, she nursed a sick sparrow back to health, and all through the summer it came to her porch to sing.

Zeidy likes animals too, even though he was kicked by a horse when he was a boy. But he's not afraid of horses. Me neither. Zeidy takes me for pony rides in the park every summer. He leads the pony and walks. I ride.

Once, on Purim, Bubby dressed up as a peddlar. She went out the back door, came round the front, and rang the bell. Zeidy didn't recognize her. He told us there was a poor lady at the door and he hurried to get his wallet so he could buy something from her. I had to hold my mouth shut tight so I wouldn't laugh out loud and spoil the fun.

At our Purim Seuda, Zeidy wears his black silk Purim-kimono — the one with the red dragon embroidered on the back — and a long, black, stovepipe hat on his head. He looks like a Jewish-Japanese Abraham Lincoln.

In our family, all the babies hear the same lullabies. Bubby sings them in Yiddish. She says *her* bubby used to sing them to *her* when she was little. When I grow up, I want to sing them to my children, too.

I think Zeidy should have been a chazan. He sings along with the chazan in shul and he hums along with the radio-tape when he's driving his car. But then he changes the tunes and shuffles them around and puts them back together in a different order. When he's finished, they sound even better than they did before!

Bubby can never find her reading glasses, so for her birthday, on Erev Pesach, I bought her a long chain to keep them around her neck. She said it was just what she needed. Now she can read the Haggada at the Seder without looking for her glasses all the time.

All the cousins and aunts and uncles come to Bubby and Zeidy for the first Pesach Seder. Every year when we find the afikoman, Zeidy looks *so* surprised! He always says, "I thought I did such a good hiding job this year. I don't understand *how* you found it!" Zeidy wears his white kittel at the Seder, the same one he wears to shul on Yom Kippur.

Shavuos is time for branches and flowers and cheese blintzes. We bring the flowers and Bubby makes the blintzes. Once, I pinned a flower on Bubby, but two tiny petals fell off and were baked right into my blintz!

On Shavuos night, Mommy and Daddy let me stay up late so I can learn in shul with Zeidy. I'm never tired, but last year, Zeidy fell asleep!

On Erev Sukkos, Bubby takes out her magic markers and her colored papers and we go to work. She draws and paints; I cut and paste. Bubby's sukka decorations are even nicer than the pictures in the museum. She makes tayglach candy too — sweet and syrupy — and puts it into a big, square, green jar. Whenever we visit her sukka, she gives me a piece. Yummy!

Zeidy's birthday is during Sukkos, so we make a sukka party for him every year. Mommy and Daddy bought him a silver esrog holder, but I bought him a pair of long, flannnel underwear because Bubby says he's cold in the winter. Zeidy said it was the best present he ever received.

Bubby never does any work while the Chanuka candles are burning. She sits on the couch and talks to us. Or she plays peek-a-boo with my baby brother. Or we play Chanuka songs on the piano and sing.

Zeidy sits on the floor with all of the cousins and plays dreidel. If he wins, he takes our pennies away and puts them in his pocket. But then, before we go home, he gives each of us a silver dollar for Chanuka gelt, so we always win more than we lose.

Don't you agree that bubbys and zeidys are super-special people? B'ezras Hashem, I'm going to be one someday — when I grow up and have children of my own, and they grow up and have children of their own. Then I can decide which I like best — being a bubby or zeidy, or being a grandchild!

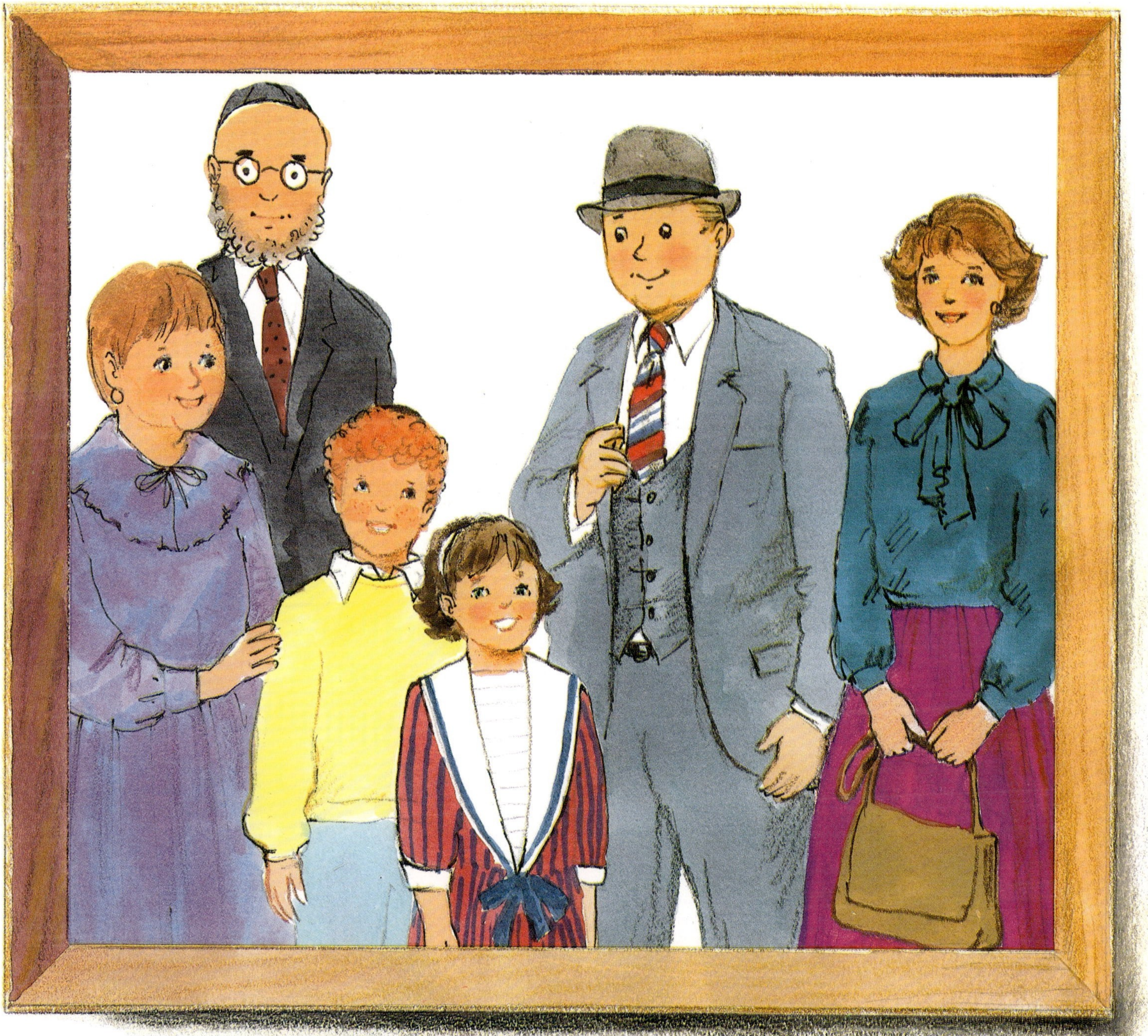

Other YAFFA GANZ books from Feldheim Publishers:

Savta Simcha and the Incredible Shabbos Bag

Savta Simcha and the Cinnamon Tree

Savta Simcha and the Seven Splendid Gifts

The Adventures of Jeremy Levi

Hello Heddy Levi

The Story of Mimmy and Simmy

Sharing a Sunshine Umbrella

Yedidya and the Esrog Tree

From Head to Toe

Who Knows One?

Follow the Moon

Shuki's Upside-Down Dream

The Terrible-Wonderful Day

The Gift that Grew

Fins, Feet, Wings and Other Animal Things

Teasers • Twisters • Stumpers

The Jewish Fact-Finder

j
306.874
Gan

```
j
306.874     Ganz, Yaffa
Gan             Me and my bubby, my
            zeidy and me
```

Withdrawn

BAKER & TAYLOR